THE NEW SUN

to Bill,
with best wishes
for your good health —
Love,
Cynthia

Also by Cynthia West from Sunstone Press.

RAINBRINGER, Poems

THE NEW SUN

POEMS   CYNTHIA WEST

SUNSTONE
PRESS

SANTA FE

Painting on front cover: *Sunflower Woman*, Cynthia West, oil on paper, 1994

Section title pages: calligraphies, Cynthia West, ink on paper, 2006

Sunstone books may be purchased for educational, business, or sales promotional use. For information please write: Special Markets Department, Sunstone Press, P.O. Box 2321, Santa Fe, New Mexico 87504-2321.

Library of Congress Cataloging-in-Publication Data

West, Cynthia, 1942-
    The new sun : poems / by Cynthia West.
        p. cm.
    ISBN 978-0-86534-582-9 (pbk. : alk. paper)
    I. Title.

PS3623.E843N49 2007
811'.54--dc22

                                    2007009000

Published in

WWW.SUNSTONEPRESS.COM
SUNSTONE PRESS / POST OFFICE BOX 2321 / SANTA FE, NM 87504-2321 /USA
(505) 988-4418 / ORDERS ONLY (800) 243-5644 / FAX (505) 988-1025

FOR THE HEALERS

CONTENTS

PREFACE

When I write poetry, the days become vividly colored. The walls melt. The canyon springs to life with screeching magpies. My neurons fire. I find myself driving a vehicle on a road leading to what I have always known. I experience the New Sun. Fresh wings allow me to communicate just what I see, the plain twigs interlaced over muddy winter paths, the smile on my daughter's cheek. They also lead me to express the unseen.

Kneeling, I retrieve shattered shards, glue them together. If I can stick even one piece to another, I have a poem. It is bread. To write poetry, I memorize suffering's names, visit the wounds no stitches can hide, gather stories in my pain bag until it bursts. Love aches if it isn't told. My words are small, round circles, elm seeds, designed to inhabit cracks. They sprout, growing leaves that house birds, blossoms that sing, shade that shelters fruit. I lean over the stream, holding a tin for panning gold, allowing water to wash away the mud until the sun flashes on wet metal. Kneeling, I retrieve shattered shards, glue them together. If I can stick even one piece to another, I have a poem. It is bread.

I offer my words to the sunrise. They are not mine to give until they have been heard and received by the light.

The silent voices, the voices of the wounded, the creatures, the clouds, the sea, the stars, and the wind ask me to speak for them. They call me to write as a pure spring issuing from stone, to nourish those who stop to drink. They give me the stories water carves in the earth, the songs of veins, capillaries, nerves, and bones.

They teach me about the buds splitting open, how their shells must rip to allow for bloom.

—Cynthia West
January 1, 2007, Santa Fe, New Mexico

1

BEGINNING

THE
FIRST
EGG
CRACK

Driven by a Hurricane

The first egg crack
thunders terror, finishes my warm float.
Surges shudder,
deafening beats increase,
signaling the end. Light shoots razor lines

spurring my furious struggle to escape,
to stretch past my small feathered bones,
ripped membranes,
strained capillaries. Suffocation. Dark. Light.

Dark. In the intense white whine
whole chunks of shell whack off,
my heart pulses faster than it can,
beak hammers a hole,
in-rushing air blasts my brain,
cold streaks rattle my lungs.

Banging, I break off more
of what I can't do without.

Driven by a hurricane
strange wet wings unfurl from panting ribs,
poke out into the air. My steaming body rises,

kicks aside the amniotic yolk
in a desperate rush
toward an eye bigger than the world.

Unfenced and Luring Colors

Challenge every pathway
you've chipped through your stone,
and your stone itself.
It is only stone because
you've labeled and held it so.

It is not stone, but rivers time failed
to catch, thousands of hooves drumming,
wind-horses,
red, yellow, white, black.

Stand unnamed
as the pearl feathers of the collared dove.
Unarmed, know there are no hunters
in this pond reflecting the sky.

Scratch in grasses,
peck kernels open, drink rainwater.
Unfenced and luring colors,
fly where no maps go.
Large breasted and voiced,
vanish between the two clouds.

Your flute demands
the feel of your breath.

Who Is It?

Stained wings, I never could be taught
how to live down here. Who is it
that goes in and out of these six sense doors,
who is it that lives in this corpse
tormented by winds?
An explorer of elm roots. Stepping back,

I feel the gold sun between my ribs,
feel hearing, feel seeing, feel grass tips
reaching higher than the window sill,
feel bird throats. Water might

come to the valley, a relief anointing
brittle crickets, a wetness
ringing trunks, vertebrae, lilies,
an infusion finding cracks in bark.

Fingers in the earth, I gather raindrops,
discover birth every moment,
death every moment. Who is it that goes?
A small seed cracking.

New Paper

New paper stretched on drying racks by the fire
        smells like wet pine needles,
        when I smooth out bumps and wrinkles.

Coyotes summon the clouds,
        chase them around the mountain,
        rousing the junipers.

My cup filled with tea reflects the rain
        outside the window. The storm has raged
        for days, polishing the cold stones.

When I pack the dried sheets
        into an ancient wooden box
        they bear marks brushed on
        by wind whirling leaves into mud,
        strokes the same color as my arm.

My cheeks feel the touch of water,
        drops fallen from a branch
        of flowering apricot
        while I made paper in a dream.
I remember the fragrance of blossoms,
        red centers surrounded by white.

Coming of Age

When the tight edges of winter hide in caves,
      the fields open diamond eyes to drink the wind.
      Friction casts sparks that eddy into flowering
      pinwheels, seeds split open
      from too much wanting.

A girl rises out of dead leaves
      at the base of the elm, skin glowing green sap.
      Growth shakes her boughs, loosens a river
      running in her. A strange water, scary in its depths,
      unfamiliar in its force, pulls her
      from the path she knows
      to stand high on a rock overlooking
      her reflection shimmering with silver fish.

With nothing on, she melts, eyes, hair
      and the notes traveling up her legs.
      She is the clouds blowing and the flood tide
      rushing to feed white-bellied buds.
      As the morning mounts,
      her visage ripples blue, gold, merging
      with the mountains, forming, dissolving.

There is no fear in her green looking,
      only amazement to find her child's eyes
      swept away by the current, drowned,
      replaced by a woman climbing
      the seven blossoms on her ladder to the sun.

The Queen's Riding Chant

Let your forgetfulness gaze
upon moonlight igniting snowy fields.
The whiteness which eats your hunger
is too dazzling to behold.
Once you swallow
this empty mirror, you can give it
to your friends. You can hold it up
to your own hate, begin the real art
of forging your crookedness
into golden circles. Practice on the cloth
you have torn apart, you will gain skill.
Clay must be separated from its mother's
body, be beaten, spun and fired, to be able
to contain water. Healing can only occur
to the broken. Guilt wears holes so joy
can shine in. Knowing your helplessness,
hold the mirror up to your disease, begin
to gallop with the Queen.

Burning Woman

The light hitting the polished floor
says, "Wake," says, "Why are you here asleep,
poor at remembering?"
The ceiling fan slices the afternoon
into theaters with many dimensions.
Wind spins reflections on the water glass,
the city, the fast traffic, the forsythia.

Your wind torn eyes see
how tall you stand, head above the turquoise sky,
orange rockets blasting. Bird flutes sound,
opening the entry gates, shimmering, free
as the wings of red-tail hawks.

Even if you hide your hands in your pockets,
they demand colors to brush on grey walls. They insist
on twining particles of ruined days into baskets
that can hold water. They are driven
to fit missing limbs into a new sort of art,
equipped for traveling the stars.

Summon the deer, call the finches
from their swift thickets. Your fingers
no longer touch the way you think they do.
Deep in the night they weave jet streams.
Waste none of your faces.
Behold your scaffold burning, cheer
your bright shaft disappearing in the sun.

One Among Many

Speed along the maze.
Gather energy to announce
your intention to enter the land
you don't know how to find.

Leaf veins are your highways.
waves carry you to shore,
pine mountains guard your search.
Your home is larger than you guess.

All night, you move as an eagle, your song
heals the torn cloak whole.

Star gifts refuse to be fenced
or let their sparks be safely staked.

The elk lends you her flute
so you can speak wearing roses.

Shielded by three dragonflies,
you come home among your plant people,
your animal people, your human people.

A small person,
one among many,
you gather ancient leaves.
You weave beauty
with every thread.

2

PRACTICES

DIGGING
THE WELL,
DAY
BY
DAY

Just Out of Reach

I must talk about digging this well
        to reach the water I am made of.
        Shovelful after shovelful, dusty rubble
        piles around. The sun rises and sets,
        unnoticed. Cloud shadows darken my face.
Ask me how long I'll be able
        to continue wearing myself out on stone,
        squandering my years
        on a tunnel into the dark.

Searching in the earth, I uncover talismans,
        that when washed and blown upon,
        remind my lost feet of the way home.
Long buried strings of deer hooves
        rattle directions I follow to read the records
        stored on the undersides of leaves.
        An oddly wrought cylinder unravels
        the day's uncertain face into strands
        more vital than anything I know.

I want only the things I can't see,
        the moon's face printed on the morning,
        the love of my friend who died.

It Will Have to Give Up

The snake has a crevice in the rock wall,
        a cave to rest in,
        motionless,
        a quiet place on an earth whirling through space.
        During how many storms will the snake

be allowed to practice stillness
        in the garden? Unable to count the mornings
        that the sun has ignited its black eyes,
        it curls in perfect equipoise,
        tongue flicking in and out.
Although bright fires thrust it through time,
        it knows it will have to give up
        its cranny in the stones.

The snake is as rooted as the mountain.
        Both travel on the speeding world. Rain slides
        down scales and slopes.
        After thunder showers, when the air clears,
        the snake slithers down its hole, shedding
        translucent skin.

Curious at the Edge

Something unfamiliar stirs in me,
a lost belonging.
I don't remember my wings, black above white snow.
Without doors, I can see landscape in my eyes,
gnarled limbs, the smell of peeled bark.

Hungry weeds, tight strings of instruments,
catch the sun along the road.
I lean, following the small sounds of bells,
joining the marks of ravens underneath plums
struggling to bloom in the dust.

Magician winds force my skin to admit
its lonely, worn strands. Cobwebs in a cup
obscure a painted deer. Birds waiting in the rafters
weave songs into crowns. Stone faces watch
footsteps fading into night.

Curious at the edge, I pretend not to notice
the road has disappeared. One finger at a time,
raindrops lick the undersides of leaves.
Keeping my eyes on the earth with each breath,
I count my feathers.

There Is No Somewhere Else

Ask me where I'm going.
I must talk about the capillaries marking the desert,
dry maps carved by water long ago.
As the day moon smiles on chessboards of fields
and the ocean falls from sight, I speed east
over wrinkled mountain breasts,
aware of the cold edge approaching.

Ask me how I am learning to walk.
By allowing the clouds to lead the way,
by holding my hands wide to catch raindrops.
I move in a brightness
beyond the small house I was taught to fit.
There is no somewhere else in the snow
hiding the pines on the mountains.

Ask me how I scale the path between the worlds,
gathering the sounds of my name
from the open-mouthed dead.
How this rented body, easily torn,
no longer matters. There is no waiting on this road,
no aloneness in this bird-filled thicket.

Ask me how my mother showed me the climb
past death, a wordless way
without bounds, a swirling river
with no banks. Nine ravens perch on the graves,
white breath laughing at the left-behind
who couldn't dare the taste for flight.

High Winds Fan the Flames

You think that by breaking you can escape
       your shadow but it is dead-set
       to devour you as soon as your wax wings
       melt. Cracked glass running across the desert
       shatters in the sun. Rain comes rarely,
       cauterizing scars. Water does not break.

Every drop of sweat and tears forms
       a fertile hollow for a seed.
       Sixty years on the border, you gather
       tattered scraps caught on thorns.
       When the scorched earth cools to blue,
       you close your eyes, patch remnants into flags
       bearing the bleached colors of hope.

When white bones speak to the moon,
       the lizards listen to the hills lifting stones.
       Gluing fast, keeping ahead of the black trail,
       your hands press, salving your gaps
       with chrysanthemums and mud.

Busy Escaping

Look how you coast high above
your worthlessness in a small plane,
specially equipped with blinders.
You built the landing gear to come down
only where you think it is safe.

Know you've been busy escaping
the rest of your life,
by a thousand contrived deaths.
Your medicine chest brims with drugs,
relief from the days peeling
your skin down to raw pain.

Rethink how you've fled the messages
trees let fall on you in all their changing leaves.
It could be it's not too late to piece together
what you do not want to hear, to listen
with the body inside your body
that receives warm sun.

Pay attention to the seeds hanging dormant
from the roof of your skull like bats.
Open the cave, let them fly free,
let them take root
in all your empty places.

Denise on Her Horse

after a painting by Catherine Ferguson, Denise on her Horse

Naked on the galloping horse,
  the white, full-fleshed woman
  opens her legs to the wind.
She couldn't have posed for this painting,
  with her head and hair trailing
  down his muscled flanks.

Dark mountains in the background,
  dark skies and flashing earth
  set off her glowing belly, a cup raised,
  offering water to the parched land.

She remembers the brush strokes
  rounding her breasts, the pauses
  between them, doors to riding the stars.

She sees herself as if asleep,
  a house being painted. Her fleeting lives
  race over the stony hills of Spain,
  glimpse lost familiar faces,
  kiss with burning speed.

Although the canvas is framed, fixed to a wall,
  there is no end to the familiar thrust
  of her momentum.

One with the rushing steed, she flies,
  her features re-made in russet, olive, ivory.
She has fallen through
  the unsuspecting light, leaving her weight.
  Agreeing. Willingly.

The Portrait Painter

To paint your portrait I must ask you
to peel away the layers of years, the coats
you have worn too long. The ideas you
smoothed over your original

eyes are not what I'm here to paint.
Be like a snake wriggling out of your
hard won masks. Leave your certain skin.
Old photos, the desert wedding circle,

must be ripped, glue from glue. Let me carry
those stories that made you matter to the fire.
The wind sweeps away yellow leaves
when they are no longer of use.

Your face by the window reflects
the silver November sun. Cactus and grasses
watch from the hill, guarding
forces hidden in your flesh.

Remove the lies you pasted
over your naked pain, the loneliness,
the uncompleted dreams. The wounded face
you do not want is what I came to paint.

There Is No End

At one moment, you are milk and amber bees.
        In the next, parades of dread clamor,
                "Stop, don't rear in the meadow,
                don't run faster than the wind."

Trapped and stumbling, you are forced
        to drink from dirty streams, to see
        your fields paved for parking lots.

Your liquid eyes,
        containing the moon-filled sea,
        are too large to understand the ropes
        binding your neck.

Don't allow the white-armed women
        to brush your mane, or braid ribbons
        where sky's fingers want to comb fire.

Let your hooves trample the saddle. Spread your wings
        on the ridge of your red-blooded kind.
        Flex wider than the dawn.

When you sing, bright knives cut
        the bit from your mouth.

You are a strong horse, meant to use
        your rippling flanks.
There is no end to the mountains.

Shadows Fall with Every Ash Leaf

We're masks, revolving, dancing blue
before dawn, tumbling
in the wind and laughing.

We're shadows, cast by the brightness
the ash leaves put on to drink the sun,
each a black wheel
turning death closer, a face opening on fear.

We're warm and beating, holding fast
to the current even as it demands
we let go. Our bodies house stars
that wear brilliance
to hide the vastness they can't bear.

There is Nowhere You Cannot Go

To pray you look up, where spiders weave messages,
where the sun lights seedpods into stars.
Our Lady walks off the adobe wall,
stands by the door garlanded with Christmas lights.
Wild sunflowers offer
seeds to finches. There is nowhere
you cannot go once you step on the path.

Joining flocks hurtling westward,
you migrate too swiftly
to be seen. A land with giant boulders
shelters your return, welcomes your wish
to spin past form, to become bluer than belief.
When you bow on the peak of Fear Mountain,
an eagle feather falls into your hand,
the gift you will speak in the world.
When you open your mouth
a thousand dawns shine,
the ones you have strung in a circle,
day by day.

3

LISTENING

VOICES
THAT
DISAPPEAR
IN
CHANGING
GREENS

Cast Spears to Crack the Shroud

Star people, shine out of the night the way
you always have. Lend your immensity to
every pebble on the garden path.
Appear simply, with nothing but your radiance,
asking no more favor than the wind rustling
wild plum leaves in the dark.
Star people, rise out of your deep sky waters,
shatter the blackness with your shining bones.

Human people, look up. Even mice,
bound to hoarding seeds
underground, surface to feed on the light.

Star people, launch your voices
to pierce the solitude.
Cast spears to crack the shroud
that smothers the earth.
Shoot burning rays to wipe out forgetfulness.

Human people, even the cedars
growing rooted in stone,
need stellar fire to breathe.

Star people, traverse the sky,
blaze stately cycles, pierce the distance
beyond imagination's wings.
Kindle the boundless in beating eyes.

Something Savored

A voice as old as stone
        whispers sounds deeper than my mind:
    water wearing cliffs to sand,
        ferns unwinding green.
Sha,
   sha,
      sha, forces my head to lower,
        to sink black and starred, softer
          than weight, more slow.
         Sha,
           sha,
             sha,
                undulates every strand.

Sliding down tunnels of bone, I shrink
    in narrow bends,
    swell through wide turns,
    at peace in not knowing,
        relieved.
No talisman can break my wind-swept fall,
    faster, into the maw.

A sleek voice, silvered and finned with rising moons
    guides my descent, fluctuates
       around curves,
a cadence immense in my ears
    pulses boundaries, soothing,
       yess,
          yess,
             yess,

something savored
before the word for taste,
when plants and creatures
were still complete
before the atom was split, before wholeness cracked
into a gaping wound.
See,
see,
see,
sighs the salmon
with a thousand eyes.

A Stretching Beyond

Stuck in the room the child stares into black autumn mud,
lulled by drops falling on the roof.
She slides down the panes with the rivulets,
into the secret cave on the shore
that hides paintings of antlered men holding lightening.
The rock bears traces of trees burned black,
red stone ground for blood, yellow flower juices
applied by flickering flame, before language separated
the meaning of rain from water.

Small eyes peer from nests, quickly disappear
into twigs woven against the storm.
The child presses her forehead to the glass, mouth open,
gazes at dusk dissolving the yard.
Although she watches, she can't find
the dancing deer, who hide because she looks.
She swoops down chutes,
choosing entry into bright trees, forgetful
of being lost. The ocean returns, and the cave
with seaweed-covered stones and blue whelks.
Her fingers hold it, wordlessly.

There is no limit to the things
night's hands join one to another.
When the rain ceases, a steady drip magnifies the silence,
not an absence, but a stretching beyond.
The girl by the window stays, rustling with wet leaves,
hearing quick mouse steps across the shingles.
The wind quietly leads her to enter the cave.

Bells Ring for San Ysidro Laborador

Neighbors file from the church,
walk the dusty hill,
recalling past springs under the new-leafed elms.
Mystery grins from the wind blown limbs,
hides where light slips into shade.
The old ones buried in the valley
are here with us, celebrating the patron saint
who germinates the corn.

Children holding their parent's hands
glance up, recognizing
a shape that disappears in changing greens
just past the limits of their sight.
I recall being one of those children,
needing no more than the dirt road,
the chollas, the smell of rocks,
the birds singing bluer than the sky.
The grasses had silver seed-heads,
that twisted bright between my fingers.

Ascending to the chapel,
I rippled out like water in a pool, lifted past
the walls and roads into a current
above the surface of the canyon
that moved wider than the mountain.
As I climbed along with the rest,
I stepped into a silent pause,
the same place that hid
what I could never look quick enough
to see.

Among Fallen Leaves

No more shots shatter the lichens.
The hunters have gone.
A silence rests, a turning
of grey branches holding the sun.
The mossy bird hides in the unseen gap
between the footfall and the earth.

No one can find this pause on purpose.
The secret slides unannounced
among yellow leaves.

If a hand reaches to touch it,
it is lost.

The Rain Speaks

I pour, pour green into roots,
roots of each grass-blade drink,
drink and are satisfied.
Satisfied, every leaf drinking,
but the highway, the highway severs the land.
Two smashed trucks. Two ambulances speed,
speed too late for the hospital,
two tow trucks, long lines of cars,
cars waiting, engines revving,

revving drivers, late for meetings. I want to wash,
to wash black roads away, to stop the roads
from eating the green hills,
hills lifted to drink water, hills
running gullies, brown rivulets joining,
little streams weaving, weaving into torrents,
torrents to remove human matchstick makings,
floods to wipe the earth.

I feed, feed you corn and pumpkins,
I call, call you with raindrops,
raindrops washing hardness from your eyes.
I spread, spread, my rainbow arms,
arch my arms, holding your traffic jams,
crushed cars, hospitals, corpses.
I pour, pour water down on you.

My Sea

I am Turquoise Woman.
When shore wind blows,
green turtles surf my western swell.
Mauna Kea's fiery eye drinks snow,
the eye sees far across my cobalt sea,
my sea with waves heaving,
my sea with whales blowing one-hundred-mile-breaths,
my sea with manes tossing thunder.

My sea wears rainbows on her breasts,
my sea with ears of cowrie shells,
my sea with eyes made of lava, glowing red.
My sea with teeth of black and white stones
      rolled back and forth by tides,
      grinding each other to sand.

My sea a well of salt,
      whose laughter flickers luminous fishes
      crossing the threshold of sight.
My sea with sun rays wound around her waist.
My sea whose fingers drown the unwary.
When my sea booms, cliffs tremble,
      I am breaking them apart.
When my sea dreams, the moon rolls inside shells.
I am Turquoise Woman.

The Dark Eyes of Summer

With no grandmother to show me,
I scratched under bushes
gathering dried cones, piling my aloneness
in circles on the dust. The rocks warmed me,
talked between winds, in a language
only for us. Opening lichened cheeks,
they led me to the river,
taught me the making of yellow leaf boats.
We sailed past the gates my mother didn't know,
into the dark eyes of summer.
Caves were given for painting and rainbows
for arching the sky.

Because I'd been orphaned, I had storerooms,
all the emptiness needed to house
the sounds of blue rubbing on blue,
the force of warm eggs hatching.

Because no one knew me, the boughs
found space to share leaf-making songs
and rides on currents of sap.
Sage walked the mountains with me,
cedar held my hand. With no grandmother
to show me, I found the river at dawn,
dove in.

The Girl Who Loves the Elk

During those years alone in the wrecking yard,
I talked to ruined cars, when I wasn't
beating myself senseless

or burying my waste toward a dubious spring.
My clumsy step broke whatever it touched.
It was then my grandmother told me

about the girl who loves the elk,
about the two wide ears that lift from her head,
about how she gives her wounds away

to stand in the glade, green and soaring
past the aspen's crowns. When the girl
who loves the elk sings to dragonflies,

her shame slides off, her crookedness
grows back to one tree, sun ignites the lake.
I remember all of the elk and all I cannot see.

4

PRAYERS AND DANCES

CIRCLES
WITHOUT
END

The Hills Are Wings

Tongue, part the waves, legs, split open
       spill all the rose seeds.
The hills are wings beating storm
from the clouds. Seeds ignite ice.
       It does not matter
       if you succeed. The Mother holds you
in hands larger than the stars,
stands overhead, guards your small, new cry.
Her hands breathe turquoise fire. You are running water
and the sound wind whispers at night.

Sleeping ants can't see this view. If you win
       or lose you will die in Her arms.
Bare branches shelter nesting ravens. Yellow eyes witness
the kisses you plant.
If you are worthy or not there is nowhere
       for you but Her blue path, the one
          you walk through the canyon at dawn.
She lets down the fringes
of Her shawl, rain, to clean you,
       to still you. Listen to the waving air.
All the cars are sleeping. There is no one but you
       in the empty field. You and the weeds
       slowly turning, you, dying and being born.

Prayer to the Holy Earth Mother

Holy Earth Mother,
cherry tree, family circle,
sacred pond mirror, passing clouds,
let my eyes and mouth learn your songs.
Fill my body with sun
until it can no longer pretend darkness.
Fill my hands with water
to extinguish the fires people start
but forget how to put out.
Fill my empty skin with the wind's secrets
so I can breathe cleanness
into the river's ears.

Small red and yellow birds, teach me how
to coax laughter from dry grasses.

Let me enter the book the sun writes
that records all that happens every day.
Let me erase the tales of harm.
Give me twelve cedar trees.
Give me twelve piñons.
My days are eagles.
Let the eagles speak through my lips.
I am nine yellow marigolds. I am the mountain.
I am the willow's shadow stroking stones.
I am nine striped lizards,
nine gardens in full fruit.

Sacred Mother, holy pond, please comfort
earth's cries. Undo her iron chains,
pour balm on her scars.

I bring you all my wounds in return.
Let my whole life kiss Your face,
Your holy water face.
Your face that mirrors passing clouds.

Helpless as Leaves under
The Moon of Ripening

Thunder walks down the mountain, awakening
hard green fruit. Helpless as leaves illumined
in the talons of the rising sun,
I am transparent green stretched
across dark veins. There's no defense
against the thousand dancing feet, the drums,
the voices drawing centuries
into circles without end.
Wider than the horizon, Turquoise Mother's face
towers from the land, overwhelming
the sky. There's no hiding
in this sudden nakedness, no body.

Hummingbirds strum from the vast shore
of beginnings. Peaches and apples blush,
their seeds rushing toward completion.
The ancestors dance, wind, cloud
and long hair flying, reuniting all who never left.
The years' faces, sun-turned
and night-blessed, open to let the stars through,
the tide beyond sound.

Feast Day at Zia

The peaches weight down the tree,
I rise with the Thunder Beings, the tree,
with blushed cheeks, majestic, unlimited,
filled with water. Today I let loose water,
filled with thunder, the chance to ripen fully.
Lightning stomps the earth so deep it drowns.
Approaching Zia Pueblo I see the drums pounding,
pulling the storm up the mesa.
Home waits in the unseen city, the one the Spaniards,
and even I, could never find, the only dry area
in the whole rain-drenched land.
Effortlessly, I am here
where I have always been.
Given a chair by the arbor,
I sit watching the dance, looking out
through pine needles and cottonwood leaves,
a deer in a tunnel of roses left by
Our Lady's Assumption. There is no end
to the sound, raised up along with her, the singers,
the drum, the rattles ascending. Her fire cloak,
a cool cloud cover, Her earth arms, Her water eyes,
give relief, no end to Her air heart.
No end to the dance, no end to us swept home together.

The Sacrament

We deer sisters dance, rank upon rank,
as the full moon ascends.
White wedding moccasins
lead long lines from dark
into light. Black mantas sway,
drums flower green, red rhythms,
gather the waters.

Evergreens in our hands,
we call, "Wake up, sleepers,
the new sun is shining,
here, in the night.
Get up. Listen. We are no longer us and others.
We are one people." Long hair swinging,
we raise our feathers, antennae woven from rain,
to catch songs from the stars.
How wide, our silver bracelets,
our turquoise leaves.

We are corn birthed in movement.
We are all the foods of the earth.

Why We Drum

For we are the rain clouds.
For we sing with our waters,
sing life into flower,
call roots to drink,
call death to crack seeds.

For our waters are light,
light to split husks.
For our branches awaken
on their journey toward fruit.

For we are the ancestors
come to answer your prayers.
We heard your tears and cornmeal.
We thank you with bountiful rain.

For some of our family throw lightning.
We sing thunder to stir your pollen.
For we want you to honor your waters.
Our drums can enter your belly.
Your belly that calls for our blessings,
so the children have plenty to eat.

5

SEPARATION, LONGING AND RETURN

COLD
FACES
PRESSED
TO THE
GLASS

Chosen to Be Full

When I was born, my mother's body
folded away from me, disappeared
in blue colder than the night.
Caged, without her to teach me to fly,
I found ways to travel from branch
to branch inside my empty nest.
Red flowers I painted on the trunk
provided nectar to my growing beak.
Winds spun my shelter, but never
tore it loose. I sang lessons learned
from sap, wove starlight
into rainbows between my bars.

A free bird asked me why I stayed,
feeding only on my own love stories.
She said, "You were chosen
to be full of friends,
to be at home on your own strong wings.
Push your way out. The door
only appears to be closed."

But I couldn't dare the pain of butterflies.

An Empty Wall

I think I see your eyes looking at me.
You are here in the room,
sitting in the chair by the window,
but far away.
I know it is my wanting that imagines
your warm gaze. Like the wind on the road
sweeping dust until bare rock shows,
this change in you has erased
all my faces. I don't know how to sit
at the table across from you,
raw stone striking sparks on raw stone.
It is an illusion I'm hearing, of you sharing
how your bones hurt inside your skin.
If I tell you my pain in return,
it is to an empty wall, one with
all the pictures taken down, rolled tightly
in a safe closet. You grew locks
when I wasn't looking.
Watching the sunflowers reach to touch the sky
I didn't notice you damming the river
that flowed between our common banks.
If I reach to touch your arm,
it is a closed door,
no longer home to my friend.
As summer rains wash the leaves with relief,
I don't know where to call for you,
or why you have gone.

Be Indecently Exposed

Smearing charcoal on newsprint, raising friction,
my nails blacken, scrubbing night into night.

I stay home alone, burning
my treasures to silence.

My wall of charred suitcases
is my barrier to rain.

What will I eat with my mouth closed
so no word can betray me?

I can't forget to gather magpie feathers
from the river that no longer runs.

The inside of my womb is all I have saved
for my own, secret mappings blacker than blood.

On that dark flesh I've drawn
wet wings, a hungry beak.

What I was given
almost died because I hid it.

I can't let sunrise come without me.
I must crawl out, be indecently exposed.

To Stop Borrowing

Ask me where I've been.
        I'll tell you, I've been agreeing
        with the ocean murmuring
        on the other side of the stone wall.

I still like to think I'm separate from the green grass,
        the gentle trees bending
        their leaves around me, this laughter
        of light and shade. The spaces

between my eyes and the swaying limbs
        are telling stories that are changing
        to my settled roots. My garden, planted
        where I mean it to be, is filled

with strange red birds. Since I don't believe
        the winds can shake hidden stories
        from the branches, I can't see
        the constellations spinning around

my head. Standing by a ladder looking up,
        I wonder how long it will take to complete
        my house. I admit, I've allowed myself
        to not know. Through with going along

because it is easier. I choose
        to stop borrowing, to start
        applying white paint to my portion
        of the sun.

My Creative Self

She walks through my liquid eyes,
no barrier, only rain, the rain that leaves
footsteps in the dust. There are no doors to her,
not my magpie ideas rattling the air,
not my movie sets built for false privacy.
There is nothing closed to her who knows me
better than my blood. It doesn't matter
if I'm asleep, she blooms with apples,
orchard grasses and light-dappled weeds.
Her silver laughter in the water from the well
awakens me to her gifts,
the spaces between branches.

I've avoided meeting her gaze too long,
have feared her ocean, the drowned down-current,
the floating away from my paltry docks.
In the colored arches where moments leave
just before they disappear, my hands touch
her silence, gilded by the afternoon.
I could hold this warmth for every breath I have,
feel its pulse circulating in my bones.
I could remember how to fly
with small blue birds.

The Well Has Not Run Dry

You are the last one who remembers the candles,
     who understands the music
     their flames sing to the family gathered
     around the table. You are the one who
     takes the flashlight out in freezing rain
     to save the green tomatoes.

Your daughters seem to have forgotten
     what it means to harvest the marigolds
     so they won't be found frozen black.
     They didn't seem to listen when you taught them
     the language of giving, about roses and the circle
     of winter hands that guards the sleeping fields.

They speak a new tongue learned from computers,
     the cold edge of not-hearing. Living in houses
     without thresholds, they can't guess how to enter.
     They need help opening the door to your kitchen.
     When you feed them, they do not give thanks.
     There are few people like you in the world anymore.

When the yellow cottonwood leaves rustle
     around your bed, when winter closes dark fingers,
     your daughters tiptoe in, light candles
     at noon. They say, "Mom, here are the last chrysanthemums.
     We gathered them for you." You can close your eyes.
     The well has not run dry.

Blindness

Stolen from the summit at birth,
I have been considered blind
because no one can understand

what I see.
They talk to me as if I'm a child
who doesn't soar the peaks daily.

Because I can't learn to speak like them,
my face travels time reflecting
their images. They cannot follow

where I go. Not realizing I dwell
in the perfect land with no missing shapes,
they kindly try to show me

the way home.
I have lost nothing,
but there is no way to explain

how I have let go of the riverbank
and allowed the current
to carry me. I watch them struggle

to keep from slipping
into the swift waters.
When I think of the years I've washed free,

I want to touch their cold faces pressed
to the glass in hopes of snatching a view.
Because they call me blind, they cannot see.

Exiled on the Shore

She was not of the city
with the long lines of cars,
not of the grey buildings that hid the sea.
No one knew what she meant
when she talked about water. They acted as if
they had not heard what she said.
They erased her as fast as she appeared,
until she came to think the great waves
were a mistake of her imagination.

One day she visited her mother
who lay in a house for the dying. Her mother
had been the first to teach her
the sea was a useless dream. They sat in silence,
because the old one could not hear.
They held hands. The surf roared.
The tides wore away the walls.
She whispered, "Mom, you could let yourself
swim away. You will know
when it is your time."
They sat together, rocked by the blue ocean.
The current washed away the city, the years.
Her mother murmured, "Yes."

6

AGING

IT'S
NOT
TOO
LATE

We Have Grown Old

The sweat fire has been lit.
We sit on top of the cliff watching
the sun walk toward the western mountains.
Houses sprawl across the land,
where they never were before.
It is the end of another August.
The cedars have grown tall.
It is the dark of the moon.
We have grown old praying.

Bleached Strands

A flag hangs in shreds from a weathered pole, limp
       unless breezes play its bleached strands.
When newly printed, it bore seven round images
       of the silent seed slipping into the shining sea,
       one in each color of the rainbow.

Another year, radishes swell. A row of coriander
       vies with elm sprouts. Red beet ribs
       support spreading leaves.
A winged spore floats, balancing. When
       the air stands still, it drops to root.

The garden was barely begun when I first saw
       the heart-seed sinking into the sea. I didn't know then
       what it meant to do that or how to allow the wind
       to carry me away, thread by thread.

Hand Marks Remain in the Plaster

Thirty years later, that September afternoon returns,
the smell of wet earth, you irritably
chopping straw, tossing it into the mix, telling me
how to do it. I wore a red bandana on my head,
rocked back and forth, my hoe scraping
water and dirt together in the wheelbarrow.
You said, "Don't think highly
of me. I'm just a simple guy."
But because you healed my illness,
buried it so deep it could never return,
you stood taller than the mountain to me.

Side by side, we threw mud
on the damp adobe wall,
smoothed it with our hands, sprayed water
from our mouths, smoothed again.
I built you so high our dried earth
could only topple, smashing us both to bits.
We couldn't fit our shards back together.

There was no way to know
I had what I wanted, until it broke.
Today I can't tell where the pieces landed.
I can only see our hand marks,
side by side on the warm wall.

To My Children

The same one as always, I sit,
      aged now under the grape vines,
      but no older than before.
My boughs have stretched
      as wide as my roots have drunk.
      Watering with the hose, feeding
      your dry places, there was no counting
      the leaves your small hands tossed to the sun.

Motherless, I became a parent
      by eating what I found in the desert,
      the wide-open sky, scant drops of rain,
      any bitter herb.
In my caring there were no nights,
      no days, just the hummingbird
      caught in bare hands and miles
      of moonlit sage.

With no door and no concern,
      I held your bodies when it snowed,
      soothed your sorrows with drum beats
               and songs. It
            seemed there was never
      enough food, yet we laughed
      as we cried. What I didn't know how to give
      didn't bother you, young candles
      too bright to care.
Today, I see myself standing in you,
      broken and whole, at once.

My House with No Doors

Stitching marigolds into clothes
I watch clouds kissing the folded hills.
How many warm oranges can I sew
Before snow erases all my steps?

Señora Alba

A woman feeling like watermelon and fresh summer sunlight,
her hips say hello as the front of the house,
       lifted by birds, catches fire with laughter.

Calling across the noise of roosters, semi-trucks, breakfast,
she waves a checkered apron stained from wiped-off tears.
       Bony dogs watch I-25 from the portal.
       Chipped dishes ring songs of the 30's,
       apricot canning, baked bread, steam, sweat.

Brushing stray hairs to her wispy bun, she asks the trees
why they can't sing all the way to the river,
       asks the open window where love went.
       The street-sweeper roars by, a moment she asks in,
seats at her oilcloth roses, serves sweet coffee.

Tomatoes blaze the Fourth of July to her dead husband,
       his salt grave. Slices of wall intersect her fountain,
       goldfish swivel in strong pushes to be heard,
       movie posters gradually peel.
Crowned with old photographs her white braids remember
       the bones of long kisses. The red dress on the scarecrow
       fades to rags.
No crops anymore, she's too worn to bend.

Earth raises arms around the careening house,
coaxes it off its wild spin with music that can't be heard.
       Dust settles.
       Señora Alba smiles with eyes of thunder.

Inseminates the Water

The storm is a herd of wind-horses flying
from the western lands. It is round, shrouding the sky
with clouds. The deluge is a rhythm of war-feet
approaching. Its shadows cause palm trees to tremble,
small creatures to burrow in holes. The thunder arouses
electric smells, drum rolls spreading,
waves shattering the solid toes of cliffs.

The onslaught is the ancestors bringing new life
on their backs. A raging elephant, ears spread wide,
trunk raised, it trumpets vehement blasts.
The torrent's thick hide has folded up the sun.
Galloping fast, it spews streamers of rain
that command the mangoes to grow.
Lightning gives fire to the sea, gives fire to the stalks,
unleashes the curves of shells.

Keeping still is in the storm, a wise grandmother
dwelling on a mountain among trees
that have weathered many floods.
She holds a leather bag of silence
with small black stones, with small white stones.
When the time is right
she will send the yellow-beaked bird to call the sun.

It's Not Too Late

Every day you bring me figs from the market
and the willingness to walk together in the rain.
The mountain across the valley
speaks the words you can't tell me.
Listening to ravens migrating south,
I follow black wings that echo my need.

It could be we're not too old to start.
Your eyes tell about the doves
you send to my morning window.
Deer leap the hills to hear your flute.
Although we have lost the rainbows
and the smell of cedar after summer thunder,
it could be it's not too late
to take all our views from their frames,
to look through the faces of our drought.

After all the seasons of refusing the offered touch
we still like to think we're young.
Sitting in a restaurant overlooking the sea,
watching the sun sink in a bank of clouds,
we are puppets stuck on mechanical pedestals,
who circle, facing opposite ways.
When the motor runs down, we stretch rigid limbs,
step from our little metal cage,
to discover we can only stand
with each other's help. Let the salt breeze
turn our gazes. There is no more waiting
to know this is all we have,

the touch of fingers,
the full moon silvering fishes' backs.

Our hoarded words must be spent.
Only the new step off the cliff.

Old Mother Turtle

You keep your appointed rounds,
thudding one armored foot after another,
your rhythm
too dense for bird's fast ears.

Touch Me

Couldn't I let you touch me
with the sounds you know
not the ones I demand
but the ones you are?

A Gentleness Learned

We walk in piccolo cacophony muttering
       light, shade
       dappled, daring the pain
of trust. The clock's hands have worn circles
on our faces. Blue-whiskered thickets
       count our used up days.

A wide path slowly carved
       by the years' grieving feet
       trumpets around the hill. Wind tosses
our fitful smiles, your eyes swim
in my river. No one is home
       in our house on the ridge, only silver fish

merged in the dapple-dance,
       with no concern
       for time's wrinkled ticking.
Dry as fallen leaves, we are
minutes rushing through the skins
       we spent on the sky. Our veins

throb, water into water,
       with a gentleness learned
       from the sad seasons.
We have no more masks after our colors fall,
only bare boughs,
       clasped and shaking.

7

MOVING BETWEEN REALMS

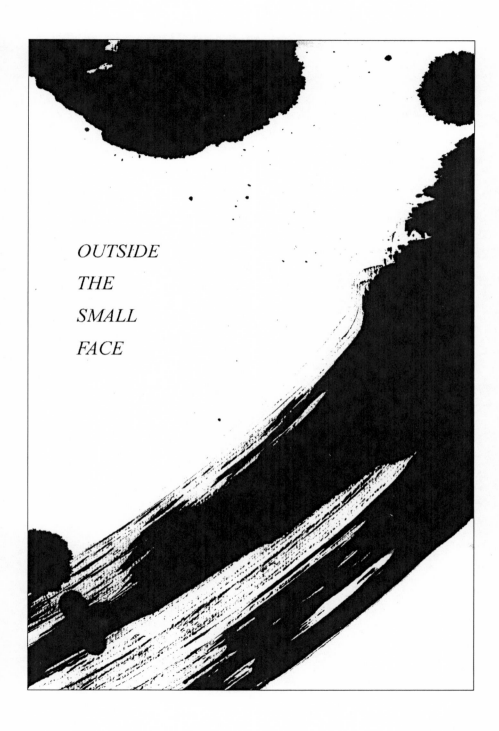

OUTSIDE

THE

SMALL

FACE

Outside the Small Face of Time

I give you the mountain standing
over my home in a green valley,
you, whose lights are flickering out.
For years I've bent, setting stone for a trail,
a place for you to put each foot. I've held you
like a mother explaining death to a child,
guided you into the familiar canyon
hidden in pine-covered hills, reassured,
"You will not be alone."

Groping along the edges, your touch defines
what you can't speak. Seeing my own eyes
in your blind guessing, I unlock
the gates barring the road to your dreams,
sweep the thresholds with twined rushes.
Traveling outside the small face of time,
I stretch your hand to reach the gifts
you have wanted so long. Your friends
at work tell you this isn't possible.

During the long winter nights I read
out loud to you, repeat the river-sounds
of your mind, lead currents of light
through the dry landscapes of your earth.
You who have chosen dying, listen.
I am your nurse, describing wings
until you believe you can fly,
until you can turn
head over heels in the air.

At the Edge of It All

A million leaves stain the twilight green.
Grass grows long. Luna moths flicker,
orange-striped and grey, wings too fast
to be glimpsed. You were kind to me

by this stone pond. The warmth of your touch
lingers in the rocks. Whispers beckon
from the gap between the trees and the sky.
The familiar ground remembers you

as the day drowns toward dark.
A circle of nothing remains, a wheel
revolving in forgotten feelings
you gave me long ago.

There are no edges to the mossy stones,
no beginning, no end,
no you, no I.
The water holds the silent moon.

Full Lunar Eclipse

It is not a cloud
but the shadow of the sun,
voracious, insatiable,
swallowing us alive.

As night deepens, ducks lose their way
in reedy shadows.
Premonitions shake the pond.

When the moon of secret fibers drinks snow,
the blood-dark cowl engulfs us,
ripping primal wails from our throats.
We beg the shrinking crescent not to leave us
alone in the dark.

Foxes, fish and falcons soundlessly
contract in hollows. Their wings
can't raise this sullen fear.

The votive candle burning in a glass
can't replace the dwindling shard,
the weeping russet drops.

Babies shudder in their sleep.
Moon of birds in thickets,
you give no promise of return.

You Have Built a Nest

In Memoriam, Frances Harwood, 1941–2003

People are leaning over you, asking how
you could have died so soon.
        They do not understand you are traveling
                in the river beneath the river
                        where all roots drink.
To them you are gone,
        not flowing up the tree.

The underground river carries your mother, carries your father,
        carries your school for restoring the earth
in its black mouth.

Your students walk away with bent backs,
                eyes cast down.
        You gave them more seeds
                than they could imagine.
Later, they will discover they know how to plant.

It is not permitted for you to speak with them
from your green latticework of boughs.

        You rise through the tree,
                in the tree you hear what the tree is saying,
                you hold the tree.

See the old iron tiller,
        ribs rusting in dry weeds.
You dug many furrows in soil, making room for sprouts.

The tree flutters with flowering stars
        in the highest branches you have built a nest
                to welcome your wild wings.

Green Iris

You died on Friday, were wrapped
in black layers of night.
Folded recluse, there's no way I can wake you.
My mouth tastes your name and I can't quit
talking to you in my head. Sunday I pray for you.
I pray Tuesday will come so I can continue
to chant your green river
that will never stop running in my veins.

Outside my window
you color me with leopard's eyes
and the emeralds, emeralds lit from within.
Your verdant face shines through the shroud,
destroying the shark's hard hide. And my view,
the green of new skies, and my throat,
the green of Buddhas,
and my breast, a green iris,
and my loins, the green of your meadows.

Inheritance

In Memoriam, John Wallace,
October 7, 1946–December 9, 2005

Your death opens all our doors,
joins us to the singing stars.

This week we bury your ashes
under the mesas. The ground
is a ladder to climb all the way up.

The moon rolls toward full
as you hand us your feathers.

We bow like the cedars,
branches silvered with the gift
of carrying on your way.

Working through us
you become a larger river,
one with no banks.

It is easy,
with your laugh.

Our Seeds Will Last Longer

The sunflower and I raise our necks
to drink the first light, to eat the valley,
the water, the field.
Standing side by side,
we sing the same song.

Roots in the earth,
prayers spiraling forward
from our stalks, our joined hands
lift to the mountain, call the clouds
to wet our lips with feathers.

Because the wind knows no time,
our seeds will last longer than days or death.
Soon, our heads will bend to face
the ground. We will watch, cold and wet.
We will turn, listening

to the horses neigh. With leaves clasped,
we will soar on wings
we know how to sound. We will lift
past the canyon,
letting our petals fall.

The Clouds Can't Keep Up

It comes from nowhere. No face. No thing.
The no-longer-me that is a flock of thrushes
slicing the morning into the sound of rain.
This open-ended tube rises

from the blue birthplace of the air.
There is nothing I can tell the rose hips
about brightness among rusting twigs.
Thousands of souls stream in and out,
leaving the mountains shaking. Change blows

so fast the clouds can't keep up.
There is no catching the speed, no holding on
to one side or the other
of the two-edged leaf.
A bird following bread crumbs

dropped in the night, I peck
my way from one white scrap to the next,
leaving tracks in the dust. Apples placed
in a circle of stones make music
no one is expected to hear.

The Orchard in Full Bloom

The herb woman buried in the 1880's
raises red blooming fingers again this spring.
The drought doesn't matter to her,
nor the traffic. Her petals ignite
the whole gnarled orchard. Bee-drunk
and wondered, even the sun falls to kiss
her fiery hands. The horses buried back then
are rising too, nothing can stay their hooves
from galloping the wind.

The santos in the church, unable to bear
the glory, leap free of nails and glue,
arise, playing mariachis.
Embracing, they celebrate
the wild plum fragrance by coupling in the grass.
The grey trunks dance, blessed
by the passion of Saint Francis and Saint Anne.
Lingering limbs explode pink flames.
Flower chambers tremble when cooing
doves enter to spark the fruit.
Every year in the orchard on this day,
death peels back to show
the new water running underneath.

8

FOREVER

INTO

THE

EYE

OF

THE

SUN

The Summer Star Circle

This is not a funeral of ravens, ravens,
but hot stomping evergreens, bodies, beat,
the beat, the Great Mother, Mother,
roses beating light, sky-spread wings.
Wings, tonight the summer circle of stars halts,
unleashes bright voices, voices forever. The mesas
gather, shoulder dark blankets, hunch, hunch
around the dance. This is not, not
the wailing of loss, but the full-throated roar
of a complete lion. Full throated dancing,
singing, singing red blood of the giving.
No sounds resound but sand grains shaking,
shooting water sparks. No one's lost
in this swollen ocean, ocean doors fly open.
Under-bellies of stones turn up watching, watching
the horizon nearing, cheering the hidden,
hidden view appearing. Ravens coax
the half moon down, down to seed our
dancing ground. This is not the ashen, ashen
dust of death, but the Great Mother's wings,
the Summer Circle, sky-spread roses,
roses brilliant in the night.

Bright, Even to the Blind

Missing the stars hidden by city lights
I start watching in a country garden.
As I look, I am seen. Forgotten flowers
return, candles bright even to the blind.

Cars roar by, raising dust.
The piñons on the hill stand witness,
branches stretched in greeting,
warm needles exhaling heat. Magpies soar,
catching the cloud's voices on their wings.

The fences that ran through the field
have long since fallen down. There is no
hindrance to the wild grass ripple dance,
the celebration of seed heads turning gold.

The stars, seeing me quiet
by the pond, give me their thousand shining eyes.
The more I open to their gaze, the more
of the night they can feed me.

As I look, I am seen. Forgotten flowers
return, candles bright even to the blind.

Baring Our Hidden Skin

We live a myth,
meeting week after week, year after year,
only to vanish in song.

Winding together in colored strands,
our voices travel deserts, which stretch
to the canyon beyond reach.

Where the river enters the sea,
we throw off our clothes,
bare our hidden skin.

Tasting the milk and honey pouring
from our mouths,
we stumble upon water.

Circling the spring,
gathering cedar, we fall
into the eye of the sun.

There is no map to this praising air,
only the cold mountain our songs
climb, note by note.

The birds teach us. Running streams
give moonlight to our tongues,
fuse our song into a silent cup.

The Flower Clouds Weaving Overhead

You ask the cactus why its green tips
fall down kissing. The earth, shaken by grasses,
knowing the answer,
blushes, too aroused to reply.

You wonder at the sound of running water
where no stream is visible. Look up
at the wind rubbing
bare limbs into leaf so hard they ripple
like rivers leaping over stones.

Don't you think the flower clouds
weaving overhead are pollinated
by finch calls and magpies? If you gaze
long enough, they will rain your eyes full
of golden drops.

You can't understand why the rocks
seem restless, wanting to stretch
inside their faces.
Put your hand on the warm ground,
it will return your touch

with violets and a thousand full moons.
There are no answers you don't know.
The wild tulip thrusts from dry leaves.
Meet it, eye to eye.

Rainbows Cast by the Plane

When the eye is too close,
        strands fail to meet.

From this distance, see
the whole earth, rust breasts running rivers,
garments of pines, jays bearing the sun
from branch to branch, prayer feathers
planted between black and white stones,
        whispers tied on twigs.

The horizon curves, holding
weeping and bullets,
        ashes spilled from a prophetic gourd.

Apricot blossoms open
        despite politicians sowing war.

Bright bees build honeycombs,
speak another tongue
        polished in the light. We keep
        storerooms of free flags, bells, and lilies.
Our house built of flowers
        will not fall.

Slowly Moving with the Sun

After the sparrow crashes into the window,
its feathered form remains imprinted
on the dusty glass. The January sun

shines through the shape, casting
a bird of light onto the floor by the stove.
I step into the beam, allow it

into my chest. Holding bruised wings
in my warmth, I stroke the little body
with the soothing sound of hearth-fire

in a snowy light. My strumming
reaches into the shaking heart,
steadying its beat. Slowly moving

with the sun to keep the brightness,
I breathe life back,
until it flies away.

In the Moon of Dead Flowers

Desert Mother, how white the doves
of your sky sing, soar me over
the turquoise border that rims bare twigs.

Desert Mother, spread your blazing orange,
your mantle, between my empty boughs.
Let your far horizon fill my sight.

Be with me, violet as the hills shadowed
by the dusk-owl's flight. When cold licks
the stones, warm me with your mouth.

Desert Mother, while grief floods your eyes,
you forgive me. I, who bandage my wounds
with promises I do not believe.

Today your wing, too soft to terrify me,
too deep to avoid, opens my shame.
Your smile rolls away miles of barbed wire.

Desert Mother, your hands
pour roses. My eyes, simple as lizards,
witness the new sun rise.

Leap with the Bobcat

There is nowhere but here to be a person,
form, fiber, bones, and fury. Howl with your maw open,
gullet exposed.
Don't dam any river. There is no time to decide
anymore. Water is needed now
along each curved artery. No weighing
and measuring. Leap with the bobcat, ear tufts alert,
eyes topaz. Listen, spread your fur wide,
let your claws take hold of shaking earth.
There is no longer solid ground,
only this split moment
caught in the boughs of dying pines.

While you are leaping, wait.
Be movement and stillness at once.
You will hear the trees crying.
Leave your racing ideas. They are too slow,
slower than the brown mouse
which lies immobile.
Pain swells, skin stretches to bursting,
everyone's fear screams.
This is today. There can be no other sound.
If it were different there wouldn't be
this muddy driveway, this hunger that calls
all night. Your breathing determines
every moment, the green ones, as well as the ones
gone stark.

There is nowhere but here
to be a person.

This book of poems is printed on acid-free paper.
The typeface is Times New Roman.
◊

Printed in the United States
74182LV00006B/355-384